How to Grow a Beanstalk

Written by Janice Vale
Illustrated by Kelly Waldek

Collins

Can you make a hard, small thing turn into a soft, tall thing?
Yes, you can.
You can grow a beanstalk. This is how!

What you need:

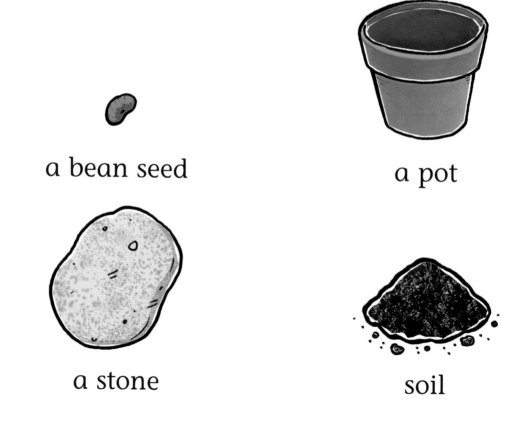

a bean seed

a pot

a stone

soil

Get a pot with a hole in the base.

Put a stone in the pot.

Put some soil in the pot.

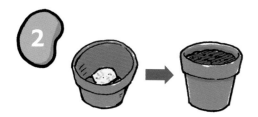

Pat down the soil.

Add some soil on top.

Pat it down so the top is flat.

4

Stand the pot on a plate.

Get it a drink from the tap. Not too much!

The soil should feel damp, not wet.

Stick a bean seed into the soil.
Put soil on top of it.
Wait for it to grow.

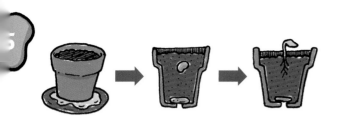

shoot

Look again in a week's time. What can you see?
Is there a shoot growing out of the soil?
Is it bending?
Look at it uncoiling.

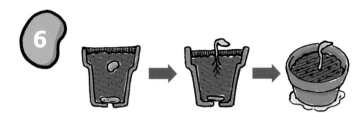

Check the soil. Is it dry?
Get it a drink from the tap.
Stand back and look at the shoot.
It is trying to get to the light.

Stand it near a window to grow.

Wait a week.

Keep checking the soil and the shoot.

Can you see a green leaf yet?

Put a stick next to the shoot.
It will curl round the stick as it gets taller.
It is turning into a beanstalk.

flower

Keep checking your beanstalk.

Look for a red flower.

Wait for the flower to die. Can you see a bean?

Keep checking and waiting.

bean seed

When the bean pod is as long as
your hand, pick it.
Cut it up and look inside.
You will see lots of seeds inside.

Save the seed and grow lots of beans next spring!

A flow chart

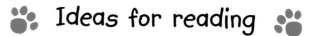

Ideas for reading

Written by Sue Graves Cert Ed (Distinction)

Learning objectives: Blend phonemes for reading; Read on sight words from texts of appropriate difficulty; Expect written text to make sense and to check for sense if it does not.

Focus phonemes: ur (curl, turning), al (beanstalk, small, tall), ow (how)

Fast words: you, a, into, what, the, some, so, should, there, of, when, your

Curriculum links: Science: Growing plants

Word count: 274

Getting started

- Write the words that feature the focus phoneme *ur*, *al* and *ow* on a small whiteboard. Ask the group to fast-read them, blending aloud if they need to.

- Write three irregular fast words on the whiteboard, e.g. *should*, *how*, *when*. Ask the children to fast-read these words. For extra practice, ask the children to write these words on their own whiteboards and show you.

- Look at the front cover together. *Do the children think this is a fiction or non-fiction book?* Ask the children to give reasons.

- Invite them to read the title together. *What might this book tell them?*

Reading and responding

- Give each of the children a copy of the book and ask them to read it independently.

- As you move around the children and listen to each child as they read, make sure that they blend the phonemes to read any words that they are unsure of.

- Ask fast-finishers to write down all the things a seed needs to grow, to share with the group at the end of the session.

- As you move round, check that children understand some of the more difficult words and phrases, e.g. *base* (p3), *uncoiling* (p7), *trying to get to the light* (p8) and *bean pod* (p12).

Edge Hill University